DOMESTIC VIOLENCE – THE SHADOW PANDEMIC

VOLUME 1, ISSUE 4 OF BRILLOPEDIA

NEHA SAMJI

ISBN 979-888530970-7

Contents

Preface

"Start writing, no matter what. The water does not flow until the faucet is turned on".

-Louis L'Amour

Hundreds of students and professors are contributing their work to Brillopedia, we are here to provide ample information about Law and Contemporary issues. Our aim is to provide a platform for today's generation to express their views and ideas on law and contemporary law.

Publication

This research paper is published in volume 1, issue 4 of Brillopedia

CHAPTER ONE

ABSTRACT

One in every three women in the world is subjected to physical or sexual violence, the majority of which is perpetrated by an intimate partner. Violence against girls and women is one of the most common Human Rights Violation. Prior to the pandemic, 243 million girls and women aged between 15 to 49 had been physically or sexually assaulted by an intimate partner in the past year. Since the pandemic, abuse of women, especially domestic violence, has multiplied manifold. Emerging reports from those on the front conveyed that all forms of violence against women and girls, particularly domestic violence, has increased since the pandemic of COVID-19. This is the Shadow Pandemic that is erupting in the midst of the COVID-19 crisis, and needs a global response to stop the same. The Domestic Violence Act is been implemented stringently in this tough times of pandemic. But certain initiatives are not been able to be taken up due to the lockdown. The major difficulty faced in these times is the communication of the violence being suffered by the victims. The abuser has to be counselled and measures should be taken to reduce the violence to the greatest extent possible. The government has to come up with various socio-legal ways to deal with this problem. The government has to put up this issue in the priority list and recognize the prevention of domestic violence as an essential service during this pandemic. Therefore, the government and the individuals have to come forward together and silence the shadow pandemic.

CHAPTER TWO

Domestic Violence Act

The Domestic Violence Act was enacted in 2005. It aims to punish the offenders and provide relief to the victims of such violence. It is the first act which defined domestic violence as well as recognized it as a human rights violation and acknowledged woman's right to live in a violence free home. In this current situation of pandemic, the Domestic Violence Act has to be analysed in a critical way and modified so as to protect those women from violence, who are not able to reach out for help due to the restrictions imposed to curb the deadly virus.

The term 'lockdown' itself gives an image of being trapped.This sense of being trapped is also accompanied with stress leading to frustration being projected on the victim at a higher degree. The lockdown has definitely provided the opportunity to the abuser in order to control and dictate all the movements and actions of their female partner, along with violence if needed. This increase in violence is not just because of frustration due to total confinement alone, as indicated through various studies. But this pandemic has also created widespread unemployment as well due to massive economic dislocation, global slowdown, closing of various businesses, etc. Often, such an unemployment is accompanied with poverty and hunger. Thus, it can be observed with reference to past data that the violence against women has increased during these times because of high unemployment, though both women and men are affected with such economic downturn, yet the women are made to suffer as well as undergo the trauma.

The women are also experiencing overburden as there work load has been increased due to all the members of the family staying at home and moreover they are being accused as well as abused for not doing their work properly. This has further resulted in more women being mentally depressed.In addition to the violation of their rights, victims of the domestic violence also face several mental as well as physical pains such as depression, chronic disorders, PTSD (post-traumatic stress disorder), sexual disorders and substance abuse. In this lockdown, due to lack of social support, the increase in susceptibility to such disorders can found in the victims of domestic violence. The children are also been prone to such a vulnerable situation during these difficult times.

"As soon as the lockdown happened, the calls at our centreswent up dramatically. We believe the number of women who are suffering are much higher because only a fraction of women who face domestic violence can actually reach out for help. Fewer still can do so during this unprecedented lockdown scenario when they don't have any respite from the tormentor and at times no opportunity to even make a call in private," said Anuradha Kapoor, founder of an NGO based in Kolkata named 'Swayam' which works for rights of women[1].

There has been a rapid rise in the number of cases of domestic violence in this lockdownacross the globe. The countries like United States, China, France, Brazil, etc. have also registered cases of intimate partner violence and rise in the cases of domestic violence. India, which has been one of the countries with a higher risk of victimization from the outset, such as dowry abuse, is experiencing a similar rise in domestic violence. Within the first face of lockdown, the National Commission of women has received around 310 grievances via mail and further more are expected to come through letters due to poor access to technology[2]. The major difficulty faced by the people locked down with their abused are that they are not able get access of internet and sometimes not even a mobile to call for help.

However, the Domestic Violence Act gives a wider scope for the victims to reach out for help in varied ways and serve them justice. In Ali Abbas Daruwala v. Shehnaz Daruwala[3], the court held that the Domestic Violence Act of 2005 is also applicable for the women governed under the Muslim Personal Law. Such a judgement squashes the ambiguity, if any and makes it clear that this law protects all those who are suffering or have gone through any kind of domestic violence, irrespective of their religion. This act also permits to provide with the shelter and monetary compensation to the aggrieved along with intermediary measures which is very much necessary during this helpless situation. In the case of Gaurav Manchanda v. Namrata Singh[4], the court granted the interm maintenance from the date of filing the substantive petition. Also, in Binita Dass v. Uttam Kumar[5], the court held that the interm maintenance cannot be denied to the wife only because she is earning or is qualified to work and earn. Later, inMegha Khandelwal v. Rajat Khandelwal and Ors.[6], the court further held that the interm maintenance apart from being granted can also be increased substantially despite the fact that the wife is well-educated. Such kind of judgements will boost the wife's confidence to complain about her husband in case of any violence caused by him as she would be getting the maintenance to feed herself as well as her children, if she feels that her income is not suffient to live away from her husband on her own self and she is not bound to suffer from such violence just because of lack of finances to live by herself.

In this time of pandemic, where the victim has to co-exist with the abuser for the time-being, atleast till the lockdown ends as she cannot be shifted to a safer place, then the online counselling sessions would surely help to curb the scale of abuse to a certain extent. Moreover, in Sabita Mark Burges v. Mark Lionel Burges[7], the court held that the respondent can be ordered to remove himself from the shared household. Such a court order is helpful in this current situation of lockdown as the wife and her children cannot be forced to leave their shared household but to prevent further domestic abuse, the husband could be moved from the house for the sake of the wife and other members of the family who are being victimised. This act also allows the court to take up Suo Moto action which can be a great help for the victims who are suffering with the violence silently. This act deals with all the major forms of abuse ranging from verbal abuse, economic abuse, physical abuse to sexual abuse. In Kasturi v. Subhas[8], the court declared that the economic abuse shall also be dealt under the Domestic Violence Act, 2005. Such judgement helps the women who are not given the right over their own earnings by their intimate partner, to claim their finances back as well as be given the right to use their earnings by themselves and for themselves.

The Domestic Violence Act has to be utilized effectively in the light of the present situation of quarantine and the people have to be made aware of the facilities which can accessed from home. It also requires to come up with various socio-legal measures to deal with the newly emerged challenges in tackling the domestic violence. A provision has to be created to put the abuser who has a long history of abuse at institutional quarantine to prevent further abuse of the victims. The victims should be provided with quick access to court and with lawyer's assistance. The government should appoint a greater number of protection officers under the Domestic

Violence Act or atleast the temporary officers should be appointed during the period of lockdown. The neighbourhood campaigns would also help to identify and protect the victims. Awareness has to be spread across the nation, highlighting the various ways to file the complaint and use the sources like news channels, radio as well as social media which helps to reach wider masses. While, there are various NGO's working towards providing medical assistance, 24/7 shelter home service, counselling, legal aid, etc. but it is also the responsibility of the government to help that such services are reached to the victims as early as possible.

The domestic violence that the women are made to go through in this society is the result of the patriarchal structure prevalent in India. Such patriarchal structure has gone too far that even in the tough times of the occurrence of a pandemic, the women are made to suffer indoors. Thereby, it is the responsibility of the government to also prioritize this issue of domestic violence and deal with it simultaneously, along with responding to Covid-19. The government has been ignoring the need to integrate domestic violence and mental health repercussions in the emergence response plans against the coronavirus. Along with the government, there is also an equal responsibility on the citizens to create awareness highlighting various modes of filing the complaints related to domestic violence. Thus, reaching out to the people facing domestic violence and other abuse has to be declared as an "essential service" by the government.

[1]SubhroNiyogi, Domestic violence on the rise in Kolkata, women fail to reach out for help, available at: https://timesofindia.indiatimes.com/city/kolkata/domestic-violence-on-the-rise-as-women-fail-to-reach-out-for-help/articleshow/75652359.cms (last visited on Nov 29, 2021).

[2]National Commission for Women, Annual Report of the Commission for 2018 - 2019 (October, 2019).

[3]2018(3)RCR(Criminal)106.

[4]258(2019)DLT314.

[5]262(2019)DLT368.

[6]MANU/SCOR/16958/2019.

[7]2013(5)BomCR387.

[8]MANU/SCOR/45031/2017.

THANK YOU

www.ingramcontent.com/pod-product-compliance
Ingram Content Group UK Ltd.
Pitfield, Milton Keynes, MK11 3LW, UK
UKHW021926190726
13853UKWH00002B/873

9 798885 309707